CATS

MAINE COON CATS

by Elizabeth Andrews

Cody Koala
An Imprint of Pop!
popbooksonline.com

This book is filled with videos, puzzles, games, and more! Scan the QR codes* while you read, or visit the website below to make this book pop.

popbooksonline.com/maine-coon

**Scanning QR codes requires a web-enabled smart device with a QR code reader app and a camera.*

abdobooks.com

Published by Pop!, a division of ABDO, PO Box 398166, Minneapolis, Minnesota 55439. Copyright ©2023 by Abdo Consulting Group, Inc. International copyrights reserved in all countries. No part of this book may be reproduced in any form without written permission from the publisher. Cody Koala™ is a trademark and logo of Pop!.

Printed in the United States of America, North Mankato, Minnesota.
102022
012023

THIS BOOK CONTAINS RECYCLED MATERIALS

Cover Photo: Shutterstock Images
Interior Photos: Shutterstock and Getty Images
Editor: Grace Hansen
Series Designer: Colleen McLaren

Library of Congress Control Number: 2022941106

Publisher's Cataloging-in-Publication Data
Names: Andrews, Elizabeth, author.
Title: Maine coon cats / by Elizabeth Andrews
Description: Minneapolis, Minnesota : Pop!, 2023 | Series: Cats | Includes online resources and index.
Identifiers: ISBN 9781098243111 (lib. bdg.) | ISBN 9781098243814 (ebook)
Subjects: LCSH: Maine coon cat--Juvenile literature. | Cat, Domestic--Juvenile literature. | Longhair cat--Juvenile literature. | Zoology--Juvenile literature.
Classification: DDC 636.83--dc23

Table of Contents

Chapter 1

Big and Fluffy

Maine coon cats are **native** to the state of Maine. Their long coats and fluffy tails are perfect for keeping them warm in cold weather.

White Maine coon cats can have eyes that are two different colors.
Watch a video here!

Maine coon cats come in different colors and patterns. Some are all white, black, or orange. Others are **tabby** or even **calico**! Maine coons usually have eyes that are green, gold, or copper.

Maine coons are one of the largest house cats. Males are 12 to 18 pounds (5–8kg). Females are 9 to 12 pounds (4–5kg). Maine coons have large, **tufted** ears. Their paws are wide and flat. This helps them walk on snow.

Maine coon cats are the official state cat of Maine.

ear
tufts
fluffy tail
large
paws

Chapter 2

Personality

Maine coon cats are gentle and kind. They are very smart. These cats get along well with kids and dogs. They stay playful even as they get older.

Learn more here!

Maine coons like to be around their people. They show lots of love and want to be a part of the action. However, not all Maine coons like to cuddle.

Chapter 3

Caring for Maine Coons

Cats are naturally clean animals. They use their tongues to clean themselves. Maine coon cats have lots of fur that needs to be brushed weekly. Their **litter boxes** should be cleaned daily.

Explore links here!

Maine coon cats are usually healthy. They should visit the vet once a year for a checkup. Cats are carnivores and need to eat food with beef, **poultry**, or fish in it.

Kittens

Maine coon kittens are born deaf and blind, like all other cats. They can hear and see around two weeks old.

Complete an
activity here!

Kittens should stay with
their mother for 12 to 16
weeks before they go to their

new homes. Maine coons
develop slowly until they are
three or four years old.

Making Connections

Text-to-Self

If you were to get a Maine coon cat, what color would you want it to be?

Text-to-Text

Have you read any other books about animals with tufted fur? What did they have in common with the Maine coon?

Text-to-World

What do Maine coon cats have in common with big cats in the wild?

Glossary

calico – (of a cat) tricolored and often including white, orange, and black.

develop – to go through the process of growth.

litter box – a box filled with cat litter, which is like sand. Cats use litter boxes to bury their waste.

native – belonging to a particular place by birth.

poultry – birds kept for eggs or meat, such as chickens, ducks, and turkeys.

tabby – (of a cat) gray or brownish in color and streaked with dark stripes.

tufted – having or growing in a tuft or tufts. A tuft is a group or clump of long strands of hair.

Index

Online Resources

popbooksonline.com

Thanks for reading this Cody Koala book!

This book is filled with videos, puzzles, games, and more! Scan the QR codes* while you read, or visit the website below to make this book pop.

popbooksonline.com/maine-coon

*Scanning QR codes requires a web-enabled smart device with a QR code reader app and a camera.